SEVEN KINDS
OF
PEOPLE
YOU FIND
IN
BOOKSHOPS

SHAUN BYTHELL

SEVEN KINDS
OF
PEOPLE
YOU FIND
IN
BOOKSHOPS

DRG

David R. Godine, Publisher

BOSTON

Published in 2020 by
David R. Godine, Publisher, Inc.
Boston, Massachusetts
www.godine.com

Simultaneously published in Great Britain by Profile Books, Ltd.

LIBRARY OF CONGRESS CATALOGING-IN-PUBLICATION DATA

Names: Bythell, Shaun, author.
Title: Seven kinds of people you find in bookshops / Shaun Bythell.
Description: Boston : David R. Godine, Publisher, 2020. |
Identifiers: LCCN 2020028387 | ISBN 9781567926927
(hardcover) | ISBN 9781567926934 (ebook)
Subjects: LCSH: Bythell, Shaun. | Antiquarian booksellers—
Anecdotes. | Booksellers and bookselling—Anecdotes.
| Book collectors—Anecdotes. | Characters and
characteristics—Anecdotes.
Classification: LCC Z325.B97 S48 2020 | DDC 381/.45002—DC23
LC record available at https://lccn.loc.gov/2020028387

NOTE: Our edition of Shaun Bythell's *Confessions of a Bookseller*
retained the author's U.K. spelling and punctuation. We have
again retained Bythell's spelling and punctuation here, so as not to
water down the text's unique vernacular.

First Printing, 2020
PRINTED IN THE UNITED STATES OF AMERICA

for Lena and Freya

CONTENTS

Introduction

IN HIS preface to *Antiquarian Books: An Insider's Account* (David & Charles, 1978) Roy Harley Lewis wrote that 'the role played by antiquarian books in world trade is, financially, quite insignificant.' That is putting a flattering spin on it. If you replace the word 'antiquarian' with 'second-hand,' then the financial impact on the global economy shifts from 'quite insignificant' to 'laughably trifling.' It was into that world that I stepped when I bought a bookshop in 2001, just four years after Amazon started selling cut-price books online. I now dream of my business making as much as even a laughably trifling dent in the global economy. In a further sign of appalling business acumen, I'm now responsible for this book, which attempts to bracket my customers unkindly into broad categories which will undoubtedly offend the very people on whom I depend for a living. This should surely seal my financial fate.

Roy Harley Lewis concludes in his preface:

'one might ask why the bookseller should be any more interesting than the shoe salesman. Yet there can be few other careers that offer such satisfaction or that make such demands as the antiquarian-book trade, requiring the dealer to play at different times the roles of detective, scholar, agent, psychologist, and fortune-teller— quite apart from that of conventional buyer and salesman.'

He may have a point. Or it may be that those of us who are singularly ill-equipped to deal with the stresses of normal life find ourselves drawn towards the business as a means of escaping from roles of the conventional 'buyer and salesman.' This isn't about us, though, the miserable, unfortunate few who have chosen to try to sell books to make a pitiful living. It is about our customers: those wretched creatures with whom we're forced to interact on a daily basis, and who—as I write this under coronavirus lockdown—I miss like long-lost friends. From the charming and interesting to the rude and offensive, I miss them all. Apart from the fact that without them I have literally no income, to my enormous surprise I have discovered that I miss the human interaction. Yesterday, a man telephoned the shop and asked for a copy of my second book, *Confessions of a Bookseller*. The total, including postage, was £18. As I was taking down his credit card details, he said, 'Please add an extra £10.' When I asked him why, he replied, 'Because I know how hard this time must be for businesses like yours, and I want you to still be there when all of this is over, so that I can come and visit the shop again.'

Others have been equally kind; I recently received a cheque from someone I've never met who told me that she'd read an article in *Time* magazine, written by Margaret Atwood, in which she encouraged people to support small businesses during this difficult time. She asked for nothing other than that I cash the cheque. The kindness of strangers can reduce you to your knees in a sobbing mess faster than a well-aimed punch to the solar plexus. This is why I miss my customers. Despite my objection to many of them, beneath their hoary exteriors there beats a kind, human heart.

The bookshops in the title of this book really only refers to my own shop. I have no wish to tarnish the reputations of others by claiming to speak on their behalf while venting my own spleen. No doubt those booksellers of a more generous disposition would paint far kinder portraits of their customers than those that follow this introduction, but these are drawn from my experiences over the past twenty years of suffering service in the trade, and I am unaware of any booksellers with a generous disposition—towards their customers, at least.

I ought also to apologise for perpetuating

stereotypes, when in reality people are far more nuanced and exist in endless subtle shades of characteristics. Generalisations are unfair, but so is life. Suck it up.

For the purposes of convenience, and of causing further offence, I've attempted to adopt a sort of Linnaean system of taxonomy, which, now that I've finished the book, I've realised doesn't really work.

1

Genus: *Peritus*

(EXPERT)

IF YOUR knowledge of Latin is as woeful as mine, then you could be forgiven for assuming (as I did) that this refers to an unsavoury part of the nether regions. It does not. It means 'expert'.

This kind of customer is—on the whole—a self-appointed expert who does not have the benefit of a regular audience on which to inflict his or her wisdom. Unlike most academics, or recognised industry commentators, who generally deal in fact-based, well-informed opinion, and who have groups of students and readers keen to hear what they have to say, most of the autodidactic types that follow have no such eager audience. As always, there are exceptions, and in their ranks can be counted some of the kindest customers I'm fortunate enough to encounter. The rest, though, are eye-wateringly tiresome.

There is nothing that the expert likes more than to use long words where short, simple language would suffice. Stamp-collecting becomes philately, looking at birds becomes ornithology and an unhealthy obsession with insects becomes entomology. It's as though they've dined out and eaten Will Self for main course followed by Jonathan Meades and Stephen Fry for dessert. The difference being that Self and Meades and Fry have all swallowed, digested and understood the full Oxford English Dictionary and know precisely how to use the correct word in the right situation to bestow clarity upon their prose, while the expert takes excruciating pains to confound the reluctant listener for nothing more than the sake of obfuscation. They know fewer than five long words, but splash them around with wild abandon for no other purpose than to create the easily-scratched veneer of intellectual superiority. But—as my pharmacist friend Cloda would say—hippopotomonstrosesquipedalianism is no excuse to make someone feel foolish for not knowing that the chemical polyvinylpyrrolidone is a binding agent in most prescription tablets.

William Faulkner and Ernest Hemingway famously argued about the use of language, with Faulkner quipping that 'Hemingway has never been known to use a word that might send a reader to the dictionary.' To which Hemingway replied, 'Poor Faulkner. Does he really think that big emotions come from big words? I know all the ten-dollar words as well as he does, but I prefer the older, simpler ones.' My

English teacher at school would have had a great deal more sympathy with Faulkner over Hemingway's use of the word 'ones,' arguing that there is no plural of the word 'one' other than 'more than one' or a higher number. He was also mercilessly pedantic about the word 'alternative,' which he maintained had its root in the Latin word 'alter' meaning one of two. It was always a source of enormous pleasure in classes to suggest that there were two alternatives. Or possibly even more.

TYPE ONE
Species: *doctus*
(SPECIALIST)

This is the kind of person who comes into the shop for no other reason than to lecture you about whatever their field of specialist interest is, and derives a singular pleasure when you know absolutely nothing about it, as you almost certainly won't. Over the years, most specialist booksellers acquire considerable knowledge which reflects their stock, but when you have a general bookshop (like mine) it is impossible to know everything. Try telling that, though, to someone who has spent their entire adult life studying the reproductive habits of the Siberian tree snail. They will sneer at you with a supercilious look of undisguised delight and contempt (in equal measure) when you reveal that no, you haven't heard of Michal Horsák's seminal work on the subject, *Mollusc Assemblages in Palaeoecological Reconstructions: An Investigation of Their Predictive Power Using Transfer Function Models*. While they derive pleasure from your ignorance of their sphere of knowledge, they are incapable of really understanding why you—or everyone else, for that matter—wouldn't want to spend twenty years living in a tent in a forest fifty miles from Omsk with a notebook and a microscope examining snail excrement, and reading nothing other than obscure academic papers on the subject.

The marginally more socially adept members of this species are conscious that other people might not share their obscure interests. This group derives an alternative sort of gratification from the fact that their niche obsession somehow differentiates them from other people, mistakenly assuming that it makes them more interesting. I used to have a regular customer who never failed to startle us by appearing at the counter without any obvious sign of having even entered the building, and cheerily announced his presence with the greeting 'Hello! I'm a bit weird, me. I love reading books about differential calculus.' The achingly obvious reality was that, in fact, he had no interest whatsoever in differential calculus but was so desperately dull that he thought that by telling people he had, it added a new dimension to his character. It didn't. It should go without saying that anyone who introduces themselves as 'a bit weird' is almost certainly not.

TYPE TWO

Species: *hominem odiosis*
(BORE)

This type of person often considers him- or herself to be a polymath, and will inveterately share their thoughts with you on any subject you choose to mention, or accidentally mention once you are aware of their proclivity. It is best to maintain complete silence when in their presence, as the slightest thing can trigger a lengthy tirade on the most unexpected of subjects, although often you don't discover that customers fall into this taxonomic category until it's far, far too late. They are not averse to listening in on conversations between other customers and interjecting with their (often wildly offensive) opinions, and on many occasions I have had to apologise to innocent bystanders who—having been quietly discussing something—have subsequently been subjected to an unsolicited (and possibly racist) rant from a complete stranger who happened to be within earshot.

We have one outstanding example of this type, and the dangers of not knowing how to deal with them are best illustrated by the following account of a day on which one of my friends offered to help in the shop.

My friend Robin appeared at eleven o'clock on a warm summer Saturday morning and took up his position behind the counter in the front of the shop. I was loitering around, pretending to work. After a couple of hours of the usual cut-and-thrust of daily bookshop life, the legendary local bore, Alfred,[1] came to the counter with three books. He thumped them down on the wooden surface with an air of serene smugness and said, with a voice dripping with entirely unjustified authority, that they were 'important books because they are responsible for the way things are now.' I have suffered sufficiently long and painfully at Alfred's hands over almost two decades to fall for this obvious attempt to invite the listener to inquire politely as to how and why these three particular books are 'important books because they are responsible for the way things are now' and thereby giving him *carte blanche* to pontificate on whatever particular prejudice or conspiracy theory is foremost in his mind that particular day, so I refused to take the bait and just smiled at him. He asked if he could leave the books on the counter while

---

1. For some reason, he's convinced himself that he's descended from King Alfred the Great, and it has been my grave misfortune to have been exposed to his wildly unlikely and frankly incomprehensible research into his genealogy over far too many years.

he went to get some cash from the bank's ATM. The moment he was out of earshot I warned Robin not to ask the question that Alfred had so obviously expected one of us to ask for fear of being on the receiving end of one of his interminable lectures on matters which he considers himself to be an authority. Which is everything. 'When he comes back to pay, don't say anything that could be construed as an interest in what he has to say' were my parting words to Robin before going upstairs to make a cup of tea, having given up on my frankly unconvincing attempt to create the illusion that I was doing something useful.

Twenty minutes later, I was in the kitchen when a battle-weary Robin appeared. He explained that Alfred had returned shortly after I'd gone, but had been unable to get cash from the ATM, so—avoiding any mention of anything that might be mistaken for interest in Alfred or his books—Robin had suggested he pay with his contactless card. 'That set him off. For the next fifteen minutes I had to listen to a paranoid monologue about cyber security. I honestly thought it might never end.'

I have yet to find a subject on which Alfred does not have a deeply unpalatable opinion, or a foreigner of whom he doesn't have an irrational fear. Inevitably, his solution to his groundless xenophobia is heavy-handed state intervention, usually involving deportation or imprisonment for the crime of nothing more than failing to share Alfred's views.

TYPE THREE
Species: *hominem utilis*
(HELPFUL PERSON)

Not all experts are a nuisance, unless—of course—you're Michael Gove. Sometimes they can be extremely useful. In January I received a telephone call from a woman in Dumfries who had been clearing out some of her library and was keen to sell some books. It was a cold, dark afternoon and when I arrived at her bungalow near the football ground I discovered boxes of books everywhere. It was an interesting and varied collection—her husband collected books about cricket, of which there were a couple of hundred, and she collected Beatrix Potter, Observer's Books and Ladybirds—all good shop stock for me. As I was going through them, I picked up an unprepossessing paperback copy of Patricia Wentworth's *Lonesome Road*, at which point she commented, 'Oh, that's an interesting book, it's extremely rare and quite valuable.' Looking at it, with its cover photo showing a box of chocolates with a syringe on top of it, I wouldn't have said that it was either rare or valuable, but she explained: 'Thorntons, the chocolate people, objected to the cover because they thought the association of their products with a syringe full of poison might damage their brand, so it was withdrawn and pulped, and another cover designed.' This sort of information is priceless to a bookseller who needs—from time to time—to convince people that he knows what he's talking about.

I have—or had until recently—a regular customer called Hamish. He died a few weeks before I finished writing this book. He was a retired actor, and had a passion for military history. He was a joy to talk to, and never short of an interesting story. He knew his subject—the Second World War—as well as any academic, but never bored or pontificated about it. He would drop gems of fascinating information briefly into our short conversations, and always leave me wanting to know more. I will miss him greatly.

TYPE FOUR

Species: *homo qui libros antiquos colligit*
(ANTIQUARIAN BOOK COLLECTOR)

The antiquarian book collector is an altogether different breed, whose interest is usually in the book as an object, rather than the information it contains, although this is not exclusively the case; many with an interest in antiquarian books use them for academic or family history research. Antiquarian collectors invariably have an encyclopaedic knowledge of the means of identifying particular editions of the books from their chosen field. For example, collectors of early editions of the works of Robert Burns, particularly *Poems, Chiefly in the Scottish Dialect*, will trawl the shelves of bookshops in search of the elusive Kilmarnock Edition, published by John Wilson of that town in 1786, armed with the knowledge that of the 612 subscription editions, only 84 are known to survive, and that they can be easily identified because Burns dedicated the book to Gavin Hamilton. They will be fully aware, too, that the second impression of the second edition (the Edinburgh Edition, of 1787, which is dedicated to 'The Noblemen and Gentlemen of the Caledonian Hunt'—Burns, the excise man, knew on which side his bannock was buttered) contains a further seventeen poems, and a misprint in 'Address to a Haggis' in which the Scots word *skinking* (meaning 'watery') was incorrectly typeset as 'stinking.' This error was perpetuated in the London Edition (also 1787), and such copies are known as the 'Stinking Editions.' This sort of arcane knowledge may seem a bit obsessive, but that's because it is, as tends to be characteristic of people who are passionate about a subject.

Another characteristic of the antiquarian subgroup of the expert is the inevitable tutting about prices. Yes, it might be a signed, limited edition two-volume set of *Ring of the Nibelung*, illustrated by Arthur Rackham, priced at £600, but you can guarantee that the customer who's pawing at it enviously will shake their head disapprovingly and tell you that they've seen it for sale considerably cheaper in another shop. It seems odd that they're looking at our copy so avariciously if this is the case. Tutting and telling booksellers that you've seen a cheaper copy is unlikely to result in a discount. We all know that sometimes we've overpaid, or that prices of particular books have fallen, but most of us are unlikely to drop a price and make a loss on a book on the word of a stranger who claims that they've seen a cheaper copy elsewhere.

I have a regular antiquarian customer who, although his bill when he comes to the counter is usually in three figures, always manages to leave you feeling as though he's robbed you the moment he's left the shop. He's retired, clearly well off, and he has an eclectic interest in rare books. The last time he was in, I had, earlier that day, bought a collection of books from a hugely entertaining elderly man whose family had clearly had both feet on one of the higher rungs of the social ladder. The books had once rested comfortably on the shelves of a stately home—they had the library stamps you always wish to see when you encounter an antiquarian book collection, with heraldic crests and a lingering smell of wood smoke from a fire stoked by a servant—but it was obvious that hard times had befallen the family, and the house had gone. I suspect these were the last remnants of the library, delivered in supermarket bread boxes. I can't remember exactly what I paid for them, but I took his contact details because there were a few things which I didn't have time to research and value, and I wanted to be able to reimburse him in the event that I had underpriced them, including a two-volume set of—I think—Malory's *Le Morte d'Arthur,* illustrated and inscribed by Aubrey Beardsley. The antiquarian came to the shop and raked through the boxes of newly acquired antiquarian stock, eventually stumbling across the Beardsley set. He asked what I wanted for it, and without the opportunity to research, I told him £800, which he (surprisingly) happily paid. Several months later, I bumped into him at a book festival in Carlisle, after which he proudly told me that he'd sold the books for £19,000 at a London auction.

As a bookseller, I feel it is incumbent on me to be fair to the people from whom I'm buying books. I felt cheated, not for me, but for the man from whom I'd bought the books. If I had put them into the same sale, and they'd made £19,000, I would have written him a cheque for most of that amount to salve my conscience. Yes, *caveat emptor*, and *caveat vendor*; we all love a bargain, but there's more to this than just money. Nobody likes to feel they've been shafted. The antiquarian knew I hadn't had the opportunity to find out more. If he'd offered to split the £19,000 with the person from whom I'd bought the books, and cut me out, I would have been more than happy.

Such encounters notwithstanding, it saddens me that the antiquarian is, it appears, a dying breed. The same could be said of most book collectors. They appear in fewer numbers each year. Information is no longer the preserve of books, and as such, books perhaps appear to be less valuable as sources than they once were. One of my parents' friends, Brian, collects books by Jeffery Farnol, an author so unfashionable that I stopped buying his books several years ago. I've told Brian as much on a number of occasions, but despite this, when he's in Scotland, he never fails to call into the shop and ask if I have any fresh Farnol in stock. He has a list, handwritten in a tatty notebook, and bursts in with an optimistic enthusiasm which I consistently fail to reflect. I never have anything he's looking for, largely because I've put all of my Farnol stock into the recycling, and it pains me to consider a future when he finally stops coming to visit. I doubt whether anyone else will ask me for Jeffery Farnol titles again until I close the door of the shop for the last time, unless he enjoys the sort of unexpected revival that Winston Graham's *Poldark* novels received following a BBC production of the series made famous by the actor Aidan Turner removing his shirt several times during each episode.

TYPE FIVE

Species: *mechanicus in domo sua*

(HOME MECHANIC)

These customers are an absolute delight. They're looking for a Haynes manual for a Land Rover, usually,
and are never disappointed when you don't have one,
and always overjoyed when you do happen to have
a copy. They don't read anything other than books
about cars, but who cares? They read what they want
to read, like everyone, and have literally nothing in the
way of literary pretensions. I love and respect them.
They are joyous in their passions and deserve nothing
but the highest praise. They will devour their literary
prey with more enthusiasm than the Oxford Profes-
sor of Early Chaucerian Manuscripts finding an early
Caxton Press piece of incunabula. And they deserve it.
They want information, and whether it's the diameter
of a spark plug for a 1947 Suffolk Punch lawnmower
or the gearbox specifications for a 1976 Ford Cortina,
it matters not. These are the people for whom movable
type ought to have been invented—the people who use
the written word to actually do something practical
with it. Not those who pretend that it was only ever
there to promote their particular flavour of religious

bigotry or confirm their belief in some sort of spurious wisdom about water-divining or dream analysis, or to convince themselves that their bungalow in Slough is at the confluence of six ley lines and, as such, should be subject to status as a national monument, when in reality it should be at the sharp end of an army of bulldozers.

The home mechanic always enters the shop nervously, and often in oily overalls, and brims with joy when you tell them that you do stock old Haynes manuals. Even if you don't have the one they're looking for in stock, they'll always find one relating to a car that one of their friends is working on. When I lived in Bristol, I had a friend who was constantly buying old cars and repairing them. He used to refer to Haynes manuals as 'The Haynes Book of Lies' because there was always some piece of wiring, or a brake fluid reservoir, which failed to match the reality of the vehicle on which he was working at that particular time.

AS FAR as the genus Peritus or Expert is concerned, on the whole, it is types one and two whom you literally want to kick out of the shop. Type one is normally just there to boast. Their husband/wife will have become so cataclysmically bored with their company over the years that they've tuned them out completely, and a bookshop provides the perfect location for them to deliver their lecture. For type two, politics is quite a popular theme. They are normally completely oblivious to the fact that their victim may not share their views, no matter how extreme. Climate change (denial, usually), same-sex marriage (disapproval, usually) and Europe (let's not go there) are their usual stock-in-trade, and the greater the indifference with which their opinions are met, the louder they feel the need to shout about them. Types three and five fall into the increasingly scarce category of people you would want to have supper with, while type four falls into the category of people who owe you several suppers, and an expensive bottle of wine, neither of which you will ever see.

2

Genus: *Familia Juvenis*
(YOUNG FAMILY)

MY FIRST Latin teacher was a Church of Scotland minister who was banished to a remote parish in the Galloway uplands—no doubt following some scandal—and who used to chain-smoke during our seemingly interminable lessons in the language. Our desks were from the 1930s and consisted of a single unit, with a cast-iron base frame on which was perched a box-like object on which you could write and in which you could store books, and a folding wooden bench that I can only assume was designed by a committee of sadists. The reason for the seat being hinged was so that when a member of staff entered the classroom, you could flip it up and move instantly from an uncomfortably seated position to an even more uncomfortable standing position to show entirely undeserved reverence to whoever had wandered into the room. The box-like part of the desk had an inkwell in the top right-hand corner—a legacy of the days of the fountain pen, but no longer required in the halcyon times of the Bic biro. This redundant feature made an ideal ashtray for the Latin teacher, and by the end of the first week of each term, every single desk in his classroom looked as though it had been adorned with an overflowing ashtray, like a table from a 1970s pub at closing time. It would be unfair to blame my appalling grasp of Latin on any of this—my lazy mind is far more likely to be the cause—but I suspect that even I might have managed to work out that *Familia Juvenis* means Young Family.

This—like every genus—has subtle (but distinct) subgroups, all of which you would be well advised to avoid. I have a young family of my own, and frequently go to considerable lengths to keep all members of it at a distance, something they appear to reciprocate. Everyone who has made the mistake of reproducing will understand this. Before I had a family of my own, I was deeply resentful of young families coming into the shop. I make great efforts to keep the shop clean, tidy and well organised. Nobody wants sticky-fingered children getting stuck into shelves, particularly when they contain rare and valuable books. Now, though, I understand. I understand both that there is nothing you can do to stop children behaving the way that they do and that their parents still want to have a tiny dose of culture in a world of nappies, Peppa Pig and vomit. I understand their reasons for bringing their children into a bookshop and leaving them in a corner so that they might escape for a minute or two and stumble across an unknown John Buchan title, or a paperback copy of Mark Twain's *The Diaries of Adam and Eve*—a book so short, so perfect and so digestible that it might as well have been written for parents of young children, whose only opportunity to read comes in the precious seconds between the wipe of an arse and a feed.

TYPE ONE

Species: *parentes lassi*
(EXHAUSTED PARENTS)

More often than not, this is a couple with several children, at least one of whom is under a year old. The purpose of their visit is—as with most of their activities—an attempt either to exhaust their children as much as their children exhaust them (mainly with pointless outdoor activities) or to find some way of distracting them so that they, the parents, can have a moment's peace. I have two sisters, and when we were young—under ten—my father, an incredibly creative and inventive man, would spend hours trying to work out a way of harnessing our childish energy (which largely manifested itself in running around, climbing in the hay barn and screaming at one another) in a way that meant we would still be happy, but which he could use to power something on the farm. In the end, I think he drew the line when he realised that his best idea was to put us all in a hamster wheel in the dairy and use the energy to run the suction pumps on the milking machines. On a rainy day, which, let's face it, is not uncommon in the south of Scotland, this is where the bookshop comes in. Our children's section—while not a patch on the children's bookshop next door—is fairly decent, and the moment they've dumped their children there, their parents can usually find something to keep them occupied for a few moments while they sneak off to the leather armchairs by the fire and slump, heads hanging, until the tranquillity is shattered by one or all of the children.

TYPE TWO

Species: *puer*

(ABANDONED CHILD)

Admittedly, this is extremely rare, but occasionally a parent—usually a father on his own—will come in with a small child, put the obliging infant in the children's section with a book, then walk slowly to the front door and quietly open it, before shouting to whoever happens to be working in the shop, 'Could you keep an eye on them? I'll be back in a minute,' and sprinting off at full tilt. Normally the 'minute' is anywhere between a quarter of an hour and an hour. On the whole, the child appears to be accustomed to this sort of thing, and will sit patiently reading until the parent returns, full of insincere apologies and unconvincing excuses. The father in this instance is usually someone whom you would least expect to desert his daughter or son. He's likely to be dressed in corduroy trousers, a nice woollen jumper (clearly not chosen by him) and a pair of shoes that would suggest that he might have a proper job; from their superior quality, evidently not one working in a bookshop.

I have a relatively new member of staff in the shop: Gillian, the Ginger Menace. She's worked here for about a year, part-time, but she bears the weighty burden of having worked in the Edinburgh branch of a shop that sells new books, during which she underwent what I am led to believe is known as 'training.' This appears to be a form of toxic brainwashing in which the victim is taught to believe all manner of nonsense, including the appalling mantra that 'the customer is always right.' She's polite, and helpful, and irritatingly industrious—characteristics that just don't cut it in a second-hand bookshop. Her principal redeeming feature is a brilliantly witty retaliatory attitude which, if folklore is to be believed, is symptomatic of her mane of ginger hair. When I told her that I was looking for stories for this book, she told me about an incident that happened in a bookshop she was working in a few years ago.

It was a busy Saturday afternoon in Edinburgh (apparently all Saturday afternoons were busy—I wish I could say the same of my business), and the shop was full of parents with children. The children's section was designed to create a comfortable environment where they might read (unlike mine, which is possibly the coldest corner of the shop, and paved with dismally un-child-friendly stone slabs). According to Gillian's account of the place, it became a haven to which parents brought their young for picnics.

On this particular Saturday the shop was unusually busy with parents and children, and one family had disappeared into the cozy reading area. Pippa, the person in charge of that part of the shop, was tidying the children's section and discovered two very young children (pre-school age) on their own. Not unreasonably, she expected that their parents had wandered off into another part of the shop, but after some considerable time there was still no sign of them, so she asked her fellow staff if anyone knew where their parents were, a question to which nobody appeared to know the answer. She sat and read to the abandoned children for some time while other bookshop employees scoured the shop in search of the errant parents with no success. Shortly before Pippa was considering calling the police, the parents appeared, excitedly clutching bags of shopping. They'd been to BHS, a fifteen-minute walk from the bookshop, and were apparently oblivious to the alarm that they'd caused, and appeared utterly perplexed by the fact that the staff in the bookshop weren't trained babysitters, part of whose job was to free them up on a Saturday afternoon to go shopping.

TYPE THREE
Species: *parentes, gloriae cupid*
(ASPIRATIONAL PARENTS)

I can tell you without the slightest shadow of a doubt that four-year-old Tarquin does NOT want to read *War and Peace*. Not all parents who want their children to achieve a high level of literacy will try to force their development, but those attempt to inflict either precociousness or misery on them. Again, in fairness, it's very rare to see, and most people are happy to let their children's reading develop at their own pace. But while I know literally nothing about child psychology, it does seem that the happiest children who come into the shop are those who are allowed to choose what books they want to read. They do, and in most cases, their parents give them the money to pay for the books themselves. This is another thing that would be all too easy to sneer at, but in an increasingly cash-free world it's a comforting thing to see that parents do this. I can only guess at the reasons, but I suspect that they're threefold: one, to teach their children how to count; two, to teach them how to interact with strangers in a controlled situation; and three, to teach them the value of money.

In the days when Nicky, the most wonderfully eccentric member of staff I've ever been fortunate enough to have employed, and one of the kindest and strangest people I've ever met, still worked in the shop we had a memorable encounter with a truly charming young family. The son—who was about seven years old—bought a copy of one of the Harry Potter books, I think, although my memory may have failed me here, and as he was paying for it, Nicky asked him what he was currently reading. He replied, '*To Kill a Mockingbird.*' Nicky was visibly taken aback, and his mother shrugged her shoulders and said, 'He chose it—we didn't think it was suitable, but he insisted.' He is obviously an exceptional child, and they were the least pushy parents I could ever have wished to meet. They don't really fit into this type, but then they don't really fit into any type. I hope to see them again.

TYPE FOUR

Species: *filii, librorum cupidi*
(BOOK-LOVING CHILDREN)

This is the inverse of the above category. I recently saw a family walking past the shop: three children ranging in age from about four to ten. As they were passing, I heard all three children clamouring and begging their parents to let them come into the shop. The mother looked in and said, 'We're not going in there, it's just a shop selling old books.' The children were clearly upset, and it doesn't trouble my conscience in the slightest to sincerely hope that their whinging continued as far as the sweet shop, and hopefully beyond. It happens in the shop, too, when non-reading parents are reluctantly dragged in by children who are keen readers. It's hard, when you're a voracious reader, to accept the fact that not everyone else is, but the reality sometimes slaps you in the face when you witness parents dragging their children out of a bookshop, rather than into it.

THE CHILDREN's section of the shop is as popular with adults as it is with children. Often it's people approaching middle age who—aware that they're not

39

getting any younger—find themselves nostalgic for their youth. Arthur Ransome, Enid Blyton, Elinor Brent-Dyer: the books of their childhoods can transport them back to that time. I'm quite sure that the success of the spoof Ladybird books is predicated on the fact that the demographic which buys them would have read the original Ladybirds as children. (Ladybird published 645 titles in the forty years prior to 1980: quite a challenge for collectors.)

The artist Miriam Elia and her brother Ezra—while not the first to spoof the old Ladybird format—did so with such success that Penguin Random House, which owns the Ladybird imprint, decided to sue her. Then, in a remarkably cynical move, they began producing the spoof titles themselves, mining their extensive archive for material and producing titles such as *The Shed*, *The Wife*, *The Meeting*, *The Hipster* and *The Ladybird Book of Mindfulness*, prompting Elia to produce (as Claire Armitstead noted in her piece in *The Guardian* from 2017) 'a poster, mocking up a book cover of an angry little girl on a toy telephone. "We sue the artist (and then rip off her idea)", her fictional publisher said. "Dung Beetle Guide to Corporate Intimidation, for ages 5+"'.

And so Elia was introduced to the world of big publishers.

3

Genus: *Homo qui meleficas amat*
(OCCULTIST)

NOBODY LIKES to be told what kind of person they are based on a deck of playing cards, or that a total stranger has access to some sort of intellectual underworld that is denied to you. These oddly elitist traits are common to all species of occultist. The occultist tends to have a bearing of smug superiority, which is a little strange, to say the least, considering their firm conviction in the utterly unbelievable. They are solitary creatures, and always visit the shop unaccompanied, although I suspect this is not through choice. They lack even the most basic social skills, and in most cases seem to have failed to grasp the rudiments of personal hygiene too. Perhaps once you have convinced yourself that you are a master of the dark arts, or that you can speak to the dead, you are entitled to adopt a fairly cavalier approach to washing, and communicating with the living. The dead, it would appear, have no sense of smell. Or style.

TYPE ONE
Species: *artifex maleficus*
(DARK ARTIST)

Always dressed completely in black, usually a bit over-weight and invariably on a quest for books by Aleister Crowley, or something antiquarian with which they believe they can summon Mephistopheles. (They've all seen *The Ninth Gate,* a much-maligned film directed by Roman Polanski in which Johnny Depp plays the role of Dean Corso, an antiquarian bookseller with dubious morals who is searching for the lost pages of an ancient satanic book for a client whose Faustian ambitions have no limits.) Dark artists—like most obsessives—are predominantly male and possessed of a look which suggests that they would be more than happy to sacrifice and/or have intercourse with a goat if they thought it would please The Great Beast. They consider those of us who sell books on the occult as unbelievers—imbeciles who don't appreciate the true existence of the fallen Lucifer as the one true god, and who consequently have failed to appreciate the inherent truth of Crowley's opportunistic goat-shag-ging orgiastic antics as the path to true enlightenment. We are lost to them. Even buying books from us is demeaning to them, because by selling these treasured texts we are commercialising the profound mysteries contained within them. And apparently it's not 'magic,' it's 'magick.' Or 'magik.'

Another type which falls into this category is the Wiccan. These people also apparently have a path to enlightenment that is unavailable to the rest of us. Stone circles appear to have considerable significance within the watered-down Wiccan blend of 'magick.' There's one near to Wigtown which is aligned to the Winter Solstice, and to which I go regularly with new visitors to the town. In my childhood it stood as nothing more than a pile of stones, imbued with the local sense that it had once been a place of historical significance, perhaps the burial place of Galdus, the first king of Galloway. In the last few years it appears to have become a good deal more than that—a place of pilgrimage where people have taken to leaving tokens. These offerings have included everything from coins to prawns, and even a half-eaten chocolate biscuit. On that occasion a visiting friend decided that it was a bit of a waste to leave the remains of the biscuit, and ate it.

It's important here to distinguish those in search of 'magick' from those interested in sleight of hand, or 'prestidigitation' as it is apparently known by those who believe that big words bestow their own kind of magic on something that everyone else considers to be little more than trickery. These are usually teenage boys, and are invariably quite charming. They are under no illusion that their form of magic is anything more than a clever trick and are usually learning the discipline to try to impress other teenagers, usually girls. Magic spells are not something they're interested in. In fact, if anything, their awareness that magic is nothing more than illusion probably precludes them from falling into the category of person who might entertain the possibility that casting spells might be a real thing.

We used to have a regular customer—a specialist dealer—who would appear (like magik) in the last week of April every year and ask for books about life after death. He'd park his black hearse in front of the shop then stagger, sweating, but confidently sweeping his few remaining strands of dyed black hair from his eyes back over his head, towards the arcane section. Every time he came to the shop he'd spend an hour pawing his way through our material, looking for books that suited his customers, then find his way to the counter and complain about our lack of stock on his subject. On one occasion—having had enough—I told him that there weren't many books written on the subject because it was, frankly, bollocks. He took a step backwards, clearly aghast, shook his head—the haunted remains of his dyed comb-over slackly slipping once again in front of his piggy eyes; tiny islands in a panda sea of cheap mascara—and mumbled something through his black lipstick which I can only assume was a curse, before walking towards the door and holding his right hand up in what appeared to be some sort of ritualistic gesture. I wonder to this day if that curse worked, and that's why I'm still working in the shop. I haven't seen him since.

TYPE TWO
Species: *homo qui coniurationes fervet*
(CONSPIRACY THEORIST)

Although not strictly speaking an occultist, the conspiracy theorist shares with the dark artist the characteristic of credulously believing in something for which there is an overwhelming body of evidence to the contrary. There is an almost infinite number of conspiracy theories, but the most frequently asked for in my shop are books about JFK's assassination and Jack the Ripper. Often the customer will ask for both. Holocaust denial and 9/11 conspiracies have been fairly popular requests recently too, often hand-in-hand. The conspiracy theorist is less easy to spot than the dark artist. At first glance—and even under scrutiny—they can appear quite normal, and are capable of sounding fairly reasonable. Alfred, for example, could almost pass for a perfectly reasonable person in appearance and conversation, provided the words 'moon landing' and 'contactless payment' are never mentioned.

If this type ever comes into the shop to sell you books, you will never be fortunate enough to find anything in which most normal people might have an interest—natural history, biography, topography or even aviation. Their boxes (or more likely black bin bags) of books will contain nothing other than books about UFOs, the Bermuda Triangle, Haitian Voodoo culture and poltergeists. For them, the highly questionable theories surrounding spontaneous human combustion are more plausible than the patently evident physics of the internal combustion engine. It is never a good idea to mock their interest, unless—of course—they've admitted that they're divesting themselves of these books because the pursuit of this arcane knowledge has proved to be a complete waste of time, and that they've finally realised that their teenage obsession with *The X-Files* was nothing more than a pubescent infatuation with Gillian Anderson which they got a bit carried away with.

TYPE THREE
Species: *homo qui cartas providas legit*
(TAROT READER)

Gazing into crystal balls and predicting the futures of complete strangers on the basis of precisely nothing has traditionally been the exclusive preserve of bearded— or at least heavily moustachioed—middle-aged types of either gender. The tarot reader fits uncomfortably neatly into this stereotype: although they encompass a broader range than the name suggests, predicting the future appears to be the leading theme in this species. Others include dream interpretation, Celtic mythology, astrology, homeopathy, Feng Shui and spiritual healing. Oh, and anything to do with crystals, provided it has absolutely no basis in science. The tarot reader is usually dressed in baggy clothes, at least one item of which must be tie-dyed. All surfaces of the tarot reader's clothes are invariably covered in dog and/or cat hair, and a trail of stale incense follows them everywhere. The tarot reader has a whiff of vagueness (as well as incense) about them but sticks rigidly to the belief that people will happily pay good money to listen to their predictions, or to be prescribed a glass of water with some sort of tincture as a cure for cancer. They often also buy books about starting your own business, but really ought to be investing in books about dealing with insolvency.

My friend Callum pretended—as a joke at university—that he could read people's futures using tarot cards. He knew absolutely nothing about it and made it up entirely, but in no time at all people were beating a path to his door for readings. Even after he admitted that he was making it all up, they still came, rather like the science fiction writer L. Ron Hubbard openly stating that he started the Church of Scientology as a means of making money and—despite this—people still believing in all the bizarre dogma and protocols he invented. As a way of attempting to convince people that he was actually making it all up, Callum's predictions became increasingly outlandish, but this seemed to serve only to feed their fervour for more until—in despair—he was forced to pretend that the power the spirits had vested in him was proving too much for him to bear, and that he could no longer continue for the sake of his health.

TYPE FOUR

Species: *venator umbrorum*

(GHOST HUNTER)

A YouGov survey in 2014 revealed that more people in the UK believe in ghosts than describe themselves as religious (34 per cent and 26 per cent respectively). More alarmingly, 9 per cent of people claim to have communicated with the dead (although technically this could include shouting at a gravestone, as it's unclear from the question whether or not the dead were required to respond). It will come as no great surprise to most people to discover that the numbers in America are considerably higher, with 45 per cent believing in ghosts and 18 per cent claiming to have had contact with one. Considering these figures, it is surprising how rarely we're asked for books about ghosts, but the customers who do ask tend to be deeply irritating. I have many *bêtes noires*–legions of them— but these must feature fairly close to the top of the list. Our otherwise excellent glossy local magazine *Dum-fries and Galloway Life* gives ill-earned column inches to a group of 'paranormal investigators' who go by the name of Mostly Ghostly. They dress—as you would expect—like extras from an extremely low-budget Dracula film, with top hats, elbow-length lace gloves, vintage dresses and chunky boots, and the results of their investigations are both wonderfully ambiguous and tiresomely inconsequential. Usually, they involve visiting a supposedly haunted house at night, turning off the lights, taking photos of old furniture and of each other and claiming to have 'felt a chill at 2.30 a.m.' or 'seen an unexplained shadow just as the sun set,' neither of which, let's face it, is particularly unusual. They don't do any harm and, if anything, provide entertainment for the gullible visitor and so, in their own way, promote the region.

If I have ever had any doubt that ghosts are nothing more than the product of troubled imaginations (and—if I'm honest, I haven't), it would come down to the fact that on four occasions customers (and staff) have independently all sensed, or have claimed to have seen, something from beyond the grave in the shop. Ordinarily I would dismiss this out of hand, but the people concerned have never met one another, nor had any reason to have communicated in any way, and all four of the 'sightings' have been in the same place: on the stairs, or on one of the landings on the stairs. While I put this down to the fact that there is probably a draught in this part of the shop, and that the light casts unusual shadows here, it has planted a seed of doubt, but the glyphosate of science has pretty much stunted its germination.

TYPE FIVE

Species: *homo artifich studiosus*

(CRAFT ENTHUSIAST)

Although not technically an occultist, craft enthusiast shares many of the characteristics of some of the subsets, most notably the tarot reader's dress sense. The craft enthusiast is never quite sure what she's looking for (they are—for the most part—women) and evades scrutiny like a well-trained spy. Even the most hardened of Stasi officers would fail to elicit exactly what sort of craft it is that the craft enthusiast thinks she's interested in. The craft section in my shop is packed with books about utterly useless time-wasting activities ranging from painting stones to knitting with dog hair. There are some practical books in there too—sewing, pottery and that sort of thing—but the craft enthusiast never, ever, buys anything useful. The craft enthusiast is usually an empty-nester, or retired—another trait shared with the tarot reader—and is looking to fill the void with something—anything. This is precisely the problem: for craft enthusiast doesn't quite know what it is that they want to do: stick-making, sugar-craft and embroidery all feature heavily when they ask for books on subjects, but there's never quite the right book for them, regardless of how many we have in stock. In a sense, not knowing fulfils its own purpose in as much as they can while away the long, lonely hours pestering unfortunate booksellers in search of fulfilment.

Not long ago, possibly three or four years, I bought the collection of a craft enthusiast, although, unusually for this predominantly dilettante type, it was someone who had made a living from her craft. She'd been a teacher and had undertaken serious academic research in her field, and her book collection was excellent. After I'd bought the books, I noticed a tatty chair near the door as I was leaving. It was an unusual piece of Arts and Crafts furniture, and she'd clearly planned to re-upholster it. I commented on it, and a couple of years later she came into the shop and gave it to me. She hadn't got round to re-upholstering it and had decided that it was time to give it a new home. I was touched by her generosity and gladly accepted it, fully aware that it had now become my problem. But that was a problem which was rapidly solved when a film crew appeared shortly afterwards looking for antiques to sell at auction for a television series called *Antiques Road Trip*. The presenter offered me £20 for it. Since I'd paid nothing for it, I accepted his offer. He emailed me a few months later to tell me that it was on the next episode of the programme. It made £200 at an auction. Shortly afterwards I bumped into the woman who had given it to me. She told me that she'd watched the programme. I was expecting a stream of invective, but she was remarkably kind and philosophical about it, and told me that this is the way of old furniture: it finds its way from one person to the next, and with luck it will be cared for and appreciated.

4

Genus: *Homo qui desidet*

(LOITERER)

I F A complete stranger is hovering in your immediate surroundings this is usually legitimate cause
for concern, but if they're showing no desire to
interact with you, this is unquestionably a good thing.
But if they appear to be there without any discernible
reason, then it is natural to assume that their presence
indicates that they are there for some nefarious purpose. If you find yourself thinking this, then you're
almost certainly correct. There seem to be some people
for whom unrelenting activity is a natural condition,
and others for whom appearing to be doing literally
nothing whatsoever is their default disposition. The
loiterer falls into the latter category, and is remarkably unsettling. They seamlessly manage to combine a
certain listless quality with the illusion that they are
conducting some sort of very important business when
it is patently obvious that they are not. What is possibly most infuriating about them is that they exude a

permanent sense of being on the point of asking you a question, which means that you have to remain in their proximity in the expectation that this will happen, which it rarely does. The moment you leave, though, to put a book on a shelf, they will, but the question will be nothing to do with books—rather, they'll ask what the time is, or what's the nearest place to find a decent lunch, or—in the case of one of my most persistent and irritating loiterers—what time the next bus leaves for Newton Stewart. Sometimes, though, other than being there to waste their time and yours, they pretend that they have nothing to do, when in reality, they have a clear purpose which they are trying to conceal. The first in this list is exactly that type.

TYPE ONE

Species: *homo qui opera erotica legit*

(EROTICA BROWSER)

This is usually—but not exclusively—a man, and usually a relatively elderly one. Although I don't suspect them of salacious behaviour in the shop, they certainly dress as you might imagine a flasher, or sex pest, would. Long coats, collars turned up, hats and occasionally dark glasses. And beards—they all have beards. Groups of giggling adolescents also fall into this category, although they tend to make little effort to conceal their delight at finding books full of photographs of people performing acts of unnaturally flexible sexual activity or—better still—Japanese Shunga illustrations involving disproportionately exaggerated genitalia. The elderly men take an altogether more furtive approach to their business, often wandering into the nearby railway section, which is more tucked away and hidden. We spend a considerable amount of time moving books back from the railway section into the erotica section. In their quest for discretion, erotica browsers have even been known to swap dust jackets of books of a similar size to convince fellow customers that they were reading *The Rolling Stock of Britain's Mainline Railway Operators and Light Rail Systems* rather than *The Mammoth Book of Lesbian Erotica* (very important to get the words of that book's title in the correct order, unless you happen to have a prurient interest in mammoth lesbians, or lesbian mammoths). Customers who indulge in this practice normally have the decency to swap the dust jackets back once they've completed their examination of their subject, but not everyone does.

Several years ago, a woman came into the shop in a panic, wanting to buy her husband a present to celebrate his imminent retirement. When she told me that he'd always had an interest in Victorian industrial architecture, I showed her to the railway room, where—to her delight—she discovered a copy of Paul Karau's *Great Western Branch Line Termini*, a book about railway stations. Her excitement at discovering this was matched only by her fury two days later when she returned to tell me that her bewildered husband had discovered that the book which the jacket was concealing was actually Helen Kaplan's *The Illustrated Manual of Sex Therapy*. I can barely imagine the conversation in which she attempted to explain her gift, but if her torrent of expletives was anything to go by, I don't think that it went particularly well.

There's something rather charming about the giggling adolescents—you can hear them as you wander through the shop—desperately stuffing books back on shelves and running off in different directions as you approach them. Their parents—like the rest of us—were guilty of the same offence at that age, and would doubtless turn a blind eye to their offsprings' curiosity, but children—particularly teenagers—are filled with the terror of being caught smoking, or with pornography, or showing any signs of growing up, so they know very well how to fool adults into thinking that they're pursuing more noble literary pursuits and following their flight from the erotica section when they hear their parents approaching, convincingly arm themselves with books about medieval Scottish church history, the branch line steam railways of Gloucestershire or the pre-Second World War works of Winston

Churchill. These are the subjects on which they are now damned to receive books from their parents as Christmas presents for the rest of their lives.

One final group deserving of perhaps the most important mention in the erotica-browsing category is young women. This is the only group whose members don't run away or try to conceal their reading material, and stands perfectly happily flicking through books from the section with the same openness as if they were reading *The Complete Works of Thomas Carlyle*. This is exactly how it should be. There is no shame in reading books from the erotica section, and if old men and teenage boys feel the need to hide the fact that they have an interest in the subject, then perhaps it reflects more on social mores than the content of the literature. Although when you do find women reading books from the erotica section, they often appear to be scrutinising them with a combination of curiosity and disappointment.

I have one regular erotica browser in my shop. He always comes in under the pretence of being interested in antiquarian books, but it never takes long for him to 'wander' into the erotica section. He always wears a wide-brimmed hat, of the sort that Crocodile Dundee wore, but I very much doubt that he's ever seen a crocodile. Sometimes I wish that he had. Recently he's taken to bringing in boxes of erotica from his own collection to sell, because 'My daughters don't want to deal with it when I'm gone.' I have some sympathy with his daughters, but there is, of course, a difference between erotica and pornography. It can be a pretty blurred boundary, and one that eBay, Amazon and other online portals struggle with, but in his case I would defend him as a genuine collector of erotica. The last box he brought in to sell contained an abridged and illustrated edition of Cleland's *Fanny Hill,* dating from about 1780. It was a beautiful book, small, and its contents were clearly not intended to be made obvious from its external appearance. It contained about half-a-dozen hand-coloured copperplate illustrations. Despite the illustrations being salacious by the standards of the time of publication, they seemed almost laughably innocent by what is considered acceptable today—about as erotic as a Werther's Original advert. I can't remember what I paid him for the two or three boxes he brought in: probably £200. A couple of weeks later another book dealer came into the shop, spotted the abridged Cleland and snapped it up. He clearly had a buyer for it, as he didn't even bother to argue with my price of £150. I often wonder where these books end up, but I certainly don't judge the buyers for their interest.

TYPE TWO

Species: *cunctatio imprudens*

<small>(LOITERER WITHOUT INTENT)</small>

I've touched on this species in previous books, as with
most of the others. They are in the shop for the sole
purpose of killing time while they await the fulfilment of a prescription from the pharmacy, or while
some sort of repair is being carried out to their car in
the garage. They're stuck with nothing to do, so they
decide to spend the hour in a bookshop, where at least
they're out of the rain and can find something interesting to read during the time they're waiting. Not that
they ever buy anything. They're almost always locals,
the downside of which is that they'll want to waste
your time by gossiping about other locals. If they're
waiting for a prescription, their conversation is usually
about the medical ailments of the people in front of
them in the queue at the chemist's. Nine times out of
ten, this means a discussion about who is about to die,
and who has recently died.

My mother adores this kind of chat. She recently
appeared in the shop while Ronnie the electrician was
in. I'd messaged him several weeks previously about
some work I need to have done in the house and he'd
replied telling me that he'd been ill. He came to the
shop to discuss the work and was in the middle of

a lengthy description of his illness, which involved chest pains, breathing difficulties and a rich variety of other physical failings, when my mother called in to say hello. As soon as she heard the words 'triple heart bypass' her ears pricked up, and she made Ronnie start again from the beginning, detailing every last element of his condition.

But back to the loiterers without intent: the worst offenders in this species are undoubtedly farmers, particularly unmarried men. These poor creatures lead fairly solitary lives, often on a windswept, damp hillside up to their elbows in the southern end of whatever livestock they're farming, so human contact is something to be treasured for them. It can be a rare thing. Another consequence of their isolation is that it gives them time to think, so they usually have quite a considerable range of opinions, but no opportunities to share them. A bookshop is the perfect place in which to do this. My friend Sandy is a lovely man who farms a few fields to the south of Wigtown, but when I see him wandering towards the shop, I know that the morning is lost.

TYPE THREE

Species: *coniunx vexata*
(BORED SPOUSE)

This is not a gender-specific species. It never fails to baffle me that someone could be bored in a bookshop, with the possible exception of someone who can't read, which pretty much excludes all adults. Loath as I am to quote the creator of *Game of Thrones*, George R. R. Martin, it's hard to argue with his observation that 'a reader lives a thousand lives before he dies. The man who never reads lives only one.' Nevertheless, the bored spouse can be recognised immediately because the first thing they'll do is find the most comfortable seat in the shop and remain there until their partner has finished browsing, or becomes acutely aware that their waiting spouse's patience is a finite commodity, and one that is being rapidly exhausted. The mobile phone is a mixed blessing, but since its advent at least the bored spouse can play Candy Crush Saga to distract themselves until their partner has satisfied their craving for literature. The signals that the bored spouse has had enough are easily recognised: folded arms, plenty of sighing, frequent checking of their watch. It's probably not fair to lump them in with loiterers as a genus, but they're certainly not in the shop to buy a book, so I think the classification can remain. The bored spouse is often accompanied by a dog, which provides them with the perfect excuse to harass their other half in the relationship, complaining that the dog is bored. In most cases, the literary spouse will be more concerned about canine ennui than that of their partner, and capitulate after the statutory fifteen minutes of browsing which they're granted on these rare occasions.

TYPE FOUR
Species: *homo qui librum suum edidit*
(SELF-PUBLISHED AUTHOR)

The reason for putting this type of person in the category of loiterer is that they're impossible to get rid of until you accede to their demands. The last thing I wish to do is belittle anyone else who has written a book. My own literary endeavours have met with considerable criticism, and it's not a pleasant experience to read an online review in which a complete stranger makes assumptions about you. Besides which, self-publishing no longer carries the stigma of being 'vanity' publishing which it once did, and indeed historically it has opened doors for literary giants such as Marcel Proust: *Swann's Way*—the first volume of *Remembrance of Things Past*—was self-published.

Even Beatrix Potter self-published *The Tale of Peter Rabbit*. But while self-publishing has opened doors for some of literature's most respected figures, it has also opened the floodgates for huge numbers of literary dwarves, many of whom—in the absence of the marketing power, promotional machinery and distribution networks of a larger publisher—are left with no choice but to take on all of those roles themselves. This largely appears to involve going around bookshops, boring the pants off booksellers who really don't want to sell anything by anyone who has self-published but who eventually, reluctantly agree to take three copies on spec just to get the author out of the shop. It is a war of attrition in which they are unfairly armed with the ample time and grim determination of retired people who can see their way around your Maginot line of defence in an instant. Their books are inevitably memoirs of their working lives or stories they've written for their grandchildren. Nothing appears to bring them more delight than wasting several hours of a bookseller's time without fear of anything other than a slight dent to their ego if their book is politely rejected. It rarely is, though: attrition has won many wars. They always carry a carbon-copy receipt book, the signing of which feels like waving a white flag and bidding a guilty farewell to the Sudetenland. This is a diary entry from 2 March 2020:

'At 4.30 p.m. I came down from the snug (where I'd been catching up on emails) to see if Gillian (the Ginger Menace) was OK. As I approached the counter I could see the back of a woman with long blonde hair in a ponytail talking to her. Gillian's face looked ashen. My instinct was to return upstairs and abandon her to the obviously unwanted conversation of this woman. There was something intangibly annoying about her very presence, but foolishly I kept going, more from a sense of curiosity than chivalry. The second I arrived at the counter, Gillian took the opportunity to escape. I don't think I've ever seen her move so fast—Usain Bolt would have struggled to keep up with her. This left me to deal with the woman. The first thing I noticed was her strange mid-Atlantic accent, and the fact that she instantly told me that she'd worked for a well-known bank, as though being associated with a company which almost collapsed in 2008 under a cloud of incompetence and greed somehow lent her a degree of credibility. Over the course of the next twenty minutes she talked incessantly, not allowing me a single word. Even now I'm not entirely sure what she was talking about. There was something about the Knights Templar, some fairies and some monks. None of it made a great deal of sense, and she kept saying 'to cut a long story short' in the middle of what turned out to be an extremely long, and utterly unintelligible, narrative. At 4.50 I noticed that Gillian had sensed my frustration at being trapped by this extraordinarily dull woman, who, it eventually transpired, had written a book (I think) and seemed to think that we held the key to her finding a publisher. To my delight, Gillian started switching off lights and closing doors. I don't think either of us was able to conceal our relief when Amanda (her name is now indelibly etched in my mind, in part thanks to the several business cards she left behind) took the hint and left the shop. As soon as she'd gone, Gillian and I exchanged the kind of knowing look that inevitably follows a shared encounter with a narcissist. She told me that she'd been trapped behind the counter by her for half an hour before I came down, and that Amanda had mentioned the bank four times in the first minute, and had spoken at considerable length about how well travelled she was. She'd been to Australia, New Zealand, Israel, Somalia, South Africa ...

The icing on the cake when it comes to self-published authors trying to market their books is when they tell you 'my grand-daughter illustrated it' and 'my friends all told me they really enjoyed it.' For most booksellers, the first reaction to this situation is to say, 'I'll just go and find the boss,' and then to find the lowest paid member of staff and pass on the unenviable task of explaining that we don't want to stock their book. In my case, the boss and the lowest-paid member of staff are unfortunately the same person: me. These authors also have a habit of sneaking into bookshops and planting copies of their dreadful books in the most visible places when you're not looking. Reviews are almost always by immediate family or terrified neighbours who risk boundary wall disputes if they fail to positively endorse the author's 'extraordinary tail' (yes, tail) 'of a cat's travels around the garden'.

The only exception to the horror of the self-published author is the local historian. These people have a passion that is matched only by their humility. They usually come into the shop quietly and, with a noble sense of embarrassment, will eventually tell you that they've spent several years researching the history of an RAF base in the area, or the names on the headstones of all the local cemeteries, and mumble that they wonder if you might be interested in stocking their book, the answer to which is an emphatic 'YES.' They have engaged in hard work, research, and produced material that future generations will thank them for. Often they've spoken to and recorded the words of people who are now dead, and without their efforts vital historical information would have been lost. And not only that: these are books which will sell. Yes, perhaps not in vast numbers, but a print run of 500 copies of a book about the origins of field names of the farms on a local estate will burn off the shelves when it comes out. People are interested in these things. Admittedly only within a small geographical area, but the work of these writers is invaluable.

5

Genus: *Senex cum barba*

(BEARDED PENSIONER)

THIS GENUS includes both males and females, although it tends to be dominated by males (by a whisker). Almost everyone in this genus travels the country in motorhomes or caravans, like a swarm of geriatric locusts, complaining about everything and never buying anything. The top travelling speed is 45 mph (also favoured by farmers who cruise country roads with piles of dead sheep in the back of their pick-ups), ensuring that everyone else is perpetually late for appointments. Apparently this is the optimal speed for fuel efficiency and, coincidentally, the optimal speed for annoying people who are trying to get to work. The drivers of the motorhome rarely care about other road users because they're retired and—until they happen to require an emergency blast from a defibrillator—don't understand why other road users are in 'such a rush.' They seem to gain particular pleasure from pulling over in scenic country spots overnight, then in the morning depositing the contents of their chemical toilet on the side of the road, then moving on ten minutes before rush hour starts so that they can begin their daily routine of holding up miles of traffic once again. The bearded pensioner will—if given the opportunity—park their huge, ugly 'Crusader' motorhome (they all have names like 'Crusader' and 'Marauder') right in front of your place of business so that they can walk straight in, and obscure it from public view for as long as possible, while buying nothing.

A distant acquaintance whom I'll call Jan, because that's her name (thank you, Rikki Fulton for that classic Revd I. M. Jolly line), has a motorhome (an Autotrail Scout, apparently), which she drives so slowly that she could be overtaken by a melting glacier. Combine harvesters have been known to honk their horns when stuck behind her on country roads. I'm convinced that she has caused more lost hours of work than anything else—except Covid-19—in the past ten years. She did ask me to point out, though, that her van doesn't have a chemical toilet. Like the pope, she shits in the woods. Or is that a bear? I can never remember.

I should also mention at this juncture that both of my parents are pensioners, although neither of them has a beard. They do, however, share with some other bearded pensioners a troubled relationship with modern technology. My sister once attempted to show my father how to use his new iPad to find things online. After she'd left, he decided to use his new-found knowledge to search for the cheapest source of gravel with which to resurface their driveway. In his charming innocence, and his first use of Google, he entered the words 'cheap hardcore' into the search engine. It took us months to convince him to try using the internet again.

TYPE ONE

Species: *vestimentis strictis amictus*
(LYCRA-CLAD)

This species has a special status in the genus because— apart from the horrors of Lycra leaving very little by way of anatomical detail to the imagination—the Lycra-clad manages to slow traffic to an agonising grind with both the camper van AND bicycles, which it mounts on the back of the vehicle, with the sole purpose of frustrating anything stuck behind it. Before embarking on a cycle ride, the Lycra-clad bearded pensioner will depart from its overnight destination and drive to any free car park where it will leave its oversized vehicle occupying at least four or, if judiciously parked, five parking spaces. From this vantage point the bicycles are removed from the back of the vehicle, and much fuss is made putting on helmets, adjusting straps, fiddling with panniers, checking laces, etc. This inevitably involves bending over and other such movements which test the elasticity of the Lycra to its very limits, before—finally—the bikes are mounted and the journey begins. In total, the cycling part of the day cannot be longer than five miles, but it must not take less than five hours.

The almost impossible physical feat of averaging a speed of 1 mph on a bicycle is achieved by breaking the journey with a stop in a bookshop. During this break, the Lycra-clad pair (and it usually is a couple) will head straight to the Ordnance Survey map section, and—standing in the most inconvenient part of the shop (ideally blocking a door or passageway)—unfold every map to plot their routes for the rest of the week, before folding the maps back up the wrong way, almost certainly tearing them in at least three places. The maps are then returned to the wrong section of the map display unit, before the Lycra-clad duo leave the shop without so much as a word to the staff. Once they've gone through the obligatory ritual of checking straps, laces, etc. once more, there invariably follows a public argument, with each of them pointing their outstretched arms, fingers indignant, in different directions before they set off once more. Routes are specifically chosen for their high volume of traffic, combined with complete lack of overtaking opportunities for vehicles unfortunate enough to be stuck behind them, resulting in satisfying tailbacks that can be seen from space, and which often make headlines in the local news. Once back at their motorhome, they'll fire-up the 'Swift Avenger' and potter onwards to find somewhere nice for the night, ideally spoiling someone's view, and with a nice, clean stream into which they can empty the toxic contents of the chemical toilet the following morning.

TYPE TWO
Species: *bracas rubras gerens*
(PANTALON ROUGE)

In yet another blatant failure of my Linnaean classification system, I am forced to concede that this species does not, in fact, have a beard. The *pantalon rouge* is nearly always clean-shaven. In the case of the males, it's usually because they've been in the army (officers) or passed through some sort of institution in which facial hair is not tolerated. It is not mandatory that the trousers in question are made of corduroy, but in most cases they are. It helps if they're slightly ill-fitting, too, ideally a couple of inches too short, fully exposing the recently polished brogues. Within the male group of *pantalon rouge* there is a requirement to be either substantially overweight or very tall and lean. They are all aged over fifty-five, and have children who are stockbrokers or who are married to stockbrokers.

There is nothing casual or meandering about this species. They are not browsers. They know exactly what they want (usually military or family history, hunting or heraldry) and approach their quest for books with an alarming determination. They never check to see how much a book costs when they find it, and never flinch when you tell them how much it is, even when it's eye-wateringly expensive. With the exception of their squaddies, they have never knowingly encountered another human being who is not a fellow *pantalon rouge*, and as such, speak to one another as though everyone else in the room is also one. This has resulted in some quite awkward situations in my shop, as only a very small percentage of my customers are *pantalons rouge*s. Members of this species are rapacious carnivores, and while they have a slight understanding of the concept of vegetarianism (nephew's girlfriend is one), it tends to be limited to the fact that Hitler was a vegetarian 'and look how he turned out!' Most male *pantalon rouge* are firmly of the conviction that 'Vegan' is one of Jupiter's moons. No member of this species is complete without at least one Labrador, preferably a black one and ideally named after a historical figure, or any object connected with the armed forces. Panzer, for example, would be perfect.

Or Mauser. Actually, thinking about it, the Germans have cornered the market in this area. You're not really going to call a dog Gatling Gun or Lee-Enfield, are you, although you might get away with Winston or Monty.

The female of this species can be roughly divided into two types: indoors and outdoors. Both are utterly terrifying. Neither generally wears *pantalon rouge*, but there is unquestionably a uniform. I'm not sufficiently *au fait* with it to know who makes it, but they must have made a fortune out of it as it appears to be a mandatory sartorial requirement. It's a sort of green tartan waistcoat, made from the hardiest of tweed. It looks like the sort of thing that's tough enough to drag through a hedge backwards without damaging a single stitch. It is invariably accompanied by a waxed jacket (Barbour). The outdoor female *pantalon rouge* wears, without exception, trousers that she has almost certainly knitted herself with the wool from the pelt of a long extinct species of mammal which has been hanging on the wall of her ancestral home for several hundred years; they are sufficiently coarse that they could comfortably exfoliate a rhinoceros. Every item of her clothing is of a colour that might have been designed with no other purpose than to disguise mud, a material of which she maintains a permanent film. She has practical hair, which she cuts herself. She has one—and only one—feature in common with the tarot reader, and that is that her clothes are covered by a layer of animal hair, but in her case it is usually a mix from several pets and a variety of livestock. No weather, no matter how foul, will prevent her from walking the dogs, which she will boot out of the house if they show the slightest reluctance to be taken for a walk. She is a keen shot, rides horses and will happily skin rabbits and pluck pheasants, and these things are reflected in her literary interests when she comes into the shop. She marches towards the counter with a look in her eye that makes you want to hide, and barks one of the following words: 'Dogs,' 'Cookery' or 'Hunting.' By 'Dogs' she means books about training gun dogs. By 'Cookery' she means exclusively books about game cookery. By 'Hunting' she means books written before the hunting ban.

The indoor type of this species is normally of a more fragile build, and takes care of her appearance, but not in an obvious way. Haircuts are in London because 'you can spot a provincial haircut a mile away.' She wouldn't go near a horse, but she loves horse-racing, and her clothes are cut from an infinitely less coarse cloth than her sister, the outdoor type, with whom she gets on despite their enormous differences in personality. This is for no other reason than that they are both *pantalons rouges*. She would never dream of taking the dog for a walk, and her interests, when she comes into the bookshop and wafts dreamily around, are a light touch of Bloomsbury (particularly Virginia Woolf) with a smattering of the Mitford sisters. She would love her grandchildren to read Beatrix Potter and Helen Bannerman, but instead they 'insist on reading that dreadful David Walliams.' Nonetheless, I am grateful for the fact that she keeps my children's section ticking over with her unappreciated gifts to them.

The *pantalon rouge* will treat staff in a bookshop with a confusing combination of absolute politeness and utter and complete disdain. It is possibly the most disarming of customers you will ever encounter in the trade, filling you with both a comforting warmth and unbridled fury.

TYPE THREE
Species: *qui in parvam domum moverunt*
(DOWNSIZERS)

This is not a species you'll find in shops that sell new books, but they appear on a daily basis in second-hand bookshops, trying to convince you that their tatty old *Reader's Digest Book of the Car* is worth a fortune, or that their *Miller's Antiques Prices Guide for 1978* is a really significant milestone in English literature. Because property is relatively cheap in this part of

Scotland, a considerable number of people move here after retirement, cashing in their equity from places where house prices are higher. This brings with it its own problems, such as pressure on the healthcare system and lack of housing for younger people, but it also brings benefits—our book festival relies heavily on volunteers, and this pool of retirees is a large one whose occupants have useful skills. Retired lawyers and accountants are snapped up extremely quickly. It also means that—in most cases—people are moving into smaller homes and having to divest themselves of some of their possessions. It comes as no great surprise that, when they're getting rid of books, they choose to keep those they enjoyed the most, which inevitably means that they attempt to dump the things they don't want (or need) on us. Occasionally something interesting will come in, but it is astonishing how often people optimistically bring in copies of *The Good Pub Guide 1988*, unbound copies of *National Geographic* magazine, *The Good News Bible*, *The Friendship Book of Francis Gay* or *People's Friend Annuals*, expecting huge sums of money for books which are all, by any measure, completely worthless.

Downsizers are easy to spot because they've usually downsized their cars too, and replaced the old Volkswagen estate with something new but considerably smaller. If you see a bearded pensioner lifting a banana box full of books from the boot of a brand-new red

Nissan Micra and heading your way, the smart money will tell you that you'll hear the word 'downsizing' in the next thirty seconds. There's something that is both exultant and tragic about downsizers—they're happy because they've retired, they have time and money, and they've moved to a place they clearly love. But tragic because they're getting rid of things which obviously meant something to them once. Their children have left home, and they are—to use one of my mother's favourite phrases since she turned seventy-five—'in the minefield now,' and the place they've downsized to will probably be the place in which they die.

TYPE FOUR
Species: *avarus*
(MISER)

Once again, this might be a type which is peculiar to the second-hand bookshop, and of whose existence the vendor of new books may well be blissfully ignorant. I hope they remain so. Misers are not just mean: they're *really* mean. They are not exclusively pensioners, but even those of a significantly younger vintage who fall into this category have a whiff of mothballs and freshly pressed grey flannel about them which might prematurely catapult them into the bearded pensioner category. Everyone in the second-hand book trade will have come across the customer who thinks that buying two books is 'bulk buying.' For the miser, the concept of inflation is incomprehensible, despite the fact that they're fully cognisant of the value of their house having trebled since they bought it in 1992. A mint-condition third edition of Newton's *Principia Mathematica*, from 1726, priced at £6,000, is enough to fire them into an incandescent rage because its original price was a groat. The bookseller will be accused of all manner of indecency for demanding more than that original groat for this 'old book' and be vilified for—as was so perfectly expressed by Bernard Black in *Black Books*—'naked profiteering'.

I have a couple of customers who fall into this category, but who somehow manage to avoid the confrontational aspect of it. They're clearly married, because the moment they enter the shop they split up and avoid one another for at least an hour while they ferret away, but when they come to the counter they will each have found at least five books in the shop which have been there since 1970, and which nobody has bothered to change the price of since then. These are books which ought to be £20 each, but which—by virtue of idleness on my part, combined with the fact that we have 100,000 books in the shop—have remained priced at £1 each. I have no idea how they hunt them out, but they do so with such determination—like pigs hunting for truffles every time they visit—that I feel that I should probably offer them each a job. They're both in their sixties. He has a very thin moustache of the type that George Orwell had in his most ill-advised whiskered days. Hers is far more luxuriant, and one which—if I owned a comb—I would find it impossible to resist the urge to lean over the counter and remove the crumbs of yesterday's breakfast from while she reluctantly opens her dusty purse and seeks through her few remaining groats for payment. They don't haggle because they know that they've already found bargains, but the transaction is still an unpleasant one for me, because we all know that they've come away considerably the better from it.

6

Genus: *Viator non tacitus*

(THE NOT-SO-SILENT TRAVELLER)

CHIANG YEE, a Chinese man born in Jiuji-ang in 1903 wrote and illustrated a beautiful series of books under the *nom de plume* 'The Silent Traveller.' The first of these was *The Silent Traveller in London* (actually, it was preceded by *The Silent Traveller: a Chinese Artist in Lakeland*, but the London book set the benchmark for the subsequent series). Yee's appeal was based on his unusual way of looking at the world. He interpreted the everyday with a 'positive curiosity'; he was acutely aware that even the most mundane of activities—from washing clothes to walking dogs—could become a subject of bewildering fascination when observed through the eyes of a stranger who lacks the benefit of familiar cultural reference points. Robert Burns—as so often—appears to have been prescient. A hundred and sixty-two years prior to the publication of Chiang Yee's *The Silent Traveller in*

Edinburgh (Methuen, 1948), Burns wrote the following words in 'To a Louse':

> *O wad some Power the giftie gie us*
> *To see oursels as ithers see us!*

When copies of Yee's books come into the shop, I often wonder if he'd read Burns and was aware that the poem was inspired by the experience of sitting behind a well-respected member of the congregation in a damp Scottish church who was oblivious to the fact that her hair was infested with lice. I hope so, but either way, the gaze of strangers cannot but help illuminate the strangeness of our own habits. Yee managed to accomplish this by quiet observation. The customers you're about to encounter are not at all like that. While Yee liked to pass unnoticed, members of this species appear to go to considerable lengths to draw attention to themselves. I don't believe this is always conscious—possibly, like a nervous tic, it is the reverse—but it is always extremely annoying.

TYPE ONE

Species: *stridens*

(WHISTLER)

Sadly this type has nothing to do with the artist who immortalised his mother on canvas, but is a man (it is always a man) who is so blissfully ignorant of the fact that this habit can be deeply irritating, particularly when it is completely tuneless (it is always tuneless), that he fails to notice quite how much the people around him dislike it. I suspect that it is something peculiar to bookshops—you rarely hear people whistling on trains, or in the supermarket. Or anywhere else, really. Most often, it is an inadvertent act of social incompetence committed by people who aren't really interested in buying books and who are wandering aimlessly around the shop, and who—for some reason—have decided that whistling will make the whole experience more enjoyable both for them and for other customers. It must be an unconscious, nervous thing but—bloody hell—I wish they'd stop. Even the most withering of stares fails to have the slightest impact on their rendition of whatever it is they think that they're whistling. Occasionally you'll catch a few accidental notes in a row which you imagine you recognise, and think 'Oh, Mahler's 8th Symphony' or 'Ah, a Bond film theme tune,' but one note later you'll be proved wrong, and realise that there is nothing even remotely musical about the whistler's wind solo. If subjected to sonic analysis, I suspect that the whistler's outpourings might bear some resemblance to the mathematical concept of π—the number which never repeats itself. The whistler's dull, infuriating notes have probably—inadvertently—created the kind of work for which the avant-garde musical genius John Cage might happily have sacrificed a limb.

TYPE TWO
Species: *sternuen*
(SNIFFER)

Of all the types in this book, this is by far the one I most want to grab by the shoulders and shake. I don't—and never will—understand why some people, when afflicted by a cold, choose to sniff every three seconds rather than blow their noses. A surprising number of the people who fall into this category appear to wear anoraks. I suspect that they live in tents in their parents' gardens. Their fields of interest are varied, and you're as likely to find their snotty snouts dribbling onto the pages of an Agatha Christie novel as a copy of Thomas Hayes's 1786 (Dublin) edition of *A Serious Address on the Consequences of Ignoring Common Coughs or Colds*.

The sniffer is blissfully unaware that his (for, again, it is almost always a man) noisy metronomic nasal inhalations are both unpleasant and irritating, and will wander through the shop, or stand at his chosen section looking at books, wetly sniffing every three seconds. The timing is so precise that it is uncanny. The temptation to thrust a tissue into their limp, clammy hand is almost overwhelming, but it would be a futile exercise, as I know from bitter experience. Once, on the train from Dumfries to Carlisle, I offered to buy the snivelling man in the seat behind me a packet of tissues, and was met with a glare of such aggressive indignation that I might as well have suggested that his parents were siblings. Which I suspect they may well have been.

TYPE THREE

Species: *susurrans*

(HUMMER)

You could be forgiven for thinking that this is pretty much the same as the whistler, but it isn't. There are some fundamental differences, chief among which is that the hummer normally has the decency to make some attempt at sticking to a recognisable tune. While the whistler generates a series of notes that would confound the most complex of random number generators, the hummer prides him-(or her-)self on musical fidelity. The tune is, admittedly, usually something dreadful (think Take That, or Cliff Richard) but it is nonetheless a recognisable series of notes. That, though, does not make it any less annoying.

Occasionally there will be a hummer and a whistler in the shop at the same time, and while the optimist would hope that these two forces might cancel each other out, sadly it appears that the opposite is true: from being two small, mildly irritating sound waves they combine to form a single, devastating tsunami of aural horror.

TYPE FOUR
Species: *crepans*
(FARTER)

This can be a silent type, and more often than not, it is. In a way, there's something slightly more noble about an audible farter, though. They appear at least to have the courage of their colonic convictions. The farter usually has the manners to find a quiet, unoccupied corner of the shop in which to commit their foul offence, but occasionally—whether out of necessity or malice I don't know—they will let fire at the counter. Quite often, when I'm walking through the shop putting books on the shelves, I'll encounter a pocket of someone's freshly expelled exhaust fumes. Normally it's pretty easy to identify the culprit, but not always. If you can see anyone hurriedly scuttling away you can be reasonably confident that they are responsible.

Recently, while I was behind the counter in the shop, checking the values of some books which I'd bought from a house near Girvan, I noticed a distinctly sulphurous whiff about the air. There was only one other person in the shop, an elderly man wearing fawn slacks pulled up just below his chest and a pair of brown Crocs. He was slowly walking away from me, a benign smile on his face. We both knew that he was the culprit, but from his grin I suspect that he was brimming with pride, rather than feigning remorse. A part of me wanted to salute him for his audacity.

TYPE FIVE
Species: *reprobans*
(TUTTER)

Perhaps the most unwelcome in the shop of all the types described in this book is the tutter. It is almost as if you can double the obnoxiousness of any of the other types by discovering that—along with their other manifest flaws—they are also a tutter. The tutter emerged from the womb with an immediate air of disapproval and opprobrium. Had they been capable of speech following their genesis, they would unquestionably have had 'words' with the obstetrician, the nurses, the midwife and the cleaners in the hospital. And probably for the architect and builders too. Nothing is good enough for the tutter, and they manifest this through an almost incessant shaking of the head and disapproving clucking sound. It is like a mating call, but the call of a creature with which no creature of sound mind would wish to mate. Like some species of expert, they are actively seeking disappointment. They have no interest whatsoever in telling their friends (all of whom are fellow tutters) about good service, a nice meal or a clean toilet. On the contrary. Without a litany of things to complain about, the tutter has no conversation. I like to think that I provide a service for the tutter in my bookshop, by telling them that we don't have a copy of whatever it is they are looking for (even if we do) or by studiously ignoring their request for help until the third 'Excuse me!' is barked with such indignation that it could be heard from the other side of the street. Prices, too, provide great fodder for tutters. Everything—no matter how cheap—is 'a rip-off.' Politically, the tutter is conservative, and is convinced that the editor of the *Daily Mail* has wandered a bit far to the left.

There is literally nothing you can do to satisfy a tutter, other than to disappoint them. Not only is it extremely easy; it's also tremendously good fun. On the rare occasions when they come to the shop with books to sell (they don't tend to be great readers) they will always refuse your offer—no matter how generous—and storm out of the shop with a furious 'I'd rather give them to a charity shop than accept that.' Which, in a nutshell, typifies the tutter: a person so convinced that the world is conspiring against them that they would rather receive literally nothing for their almost worthless Jeffrey Archer collection than the £20 you've offered them out of a misguided sense of pity.

7

Genus: *Parentum historae studiosus*

(FAMILY HISTORIAN)

I'M FIRMLY of the conviction that since we are all descended from a common ancestor, family history is really not that interesting, nor important. So what if your great-grandfather was shot in the arse by a stray bullet at Ypres? If he'd discovered a cure for Weil's disease, or worked out the solution to Fermat's last theorem, then history would make sure of his place in it. The truth is that most of us live pretty unremarkable lives, and while it's nice to think that your progenitors did great things, they probably didn't. There is really nothing to be proud of in having a family tree. There's far more to be proud of if you've actually planted a tree.

From my experience in the shop, people who study their family history are usually doing so to make a point, and it's usually a fairly petty one. But ten generations is 300 years. Someone, during those three centuries, has had an affair with a butler or a maid. Someone has pissed in your gene pool, however pure you believe your lineage is.

TYPE ONE
Species: *homines mundi novi*
(AMERICANS)

Despite the irritating fact that their ancestors emigrated from somewhere in rural Scotland to somewhere in rural America four generations ago, these people remarkably still consider themselves to be Scottish. Or worse still, 'Scotch.' There is often a high-handedness about their request when they visit the shop—'Where do you keep your collection of books about the (insert any Scottish name) clan?'—as though thousands of books have been written about their family, who survived on the buried, rotting corpses of gannets in St Kilda or some other far-flung outcrop of Scotland for dozens of genetically-challenged generations. Not that this isn't fascinating—I'm mildly obsessed with the fact that anyone could have lived on that spiky rock, which appears to have been thrown into the middle of the Atlantic by a cruel deity for no other purpose than to torture its residents. But, were it part of my family history, I suspect that I would be quick to plant my roots in the new soil, rather than cling to the barren earth of the past.

The huge majority of these customers are not from St Kilda, though, but descended from disenfranchised families driven across the sea by necessity following the Clearances, both Highland and Lowland (my friend Andrew Cassell wrote a superb book about the much-overlooked latter). I'm fairly sure that what they're really looking for is some sort of evidence that they are in fact the clan chief, and that a damp ruin in Argyll is their birthright, when in fact it is manifestly obvious that their great-great-great-grandfather's status in the clan was not that of the laird but rather that of the laird's latrine cleaner. It is touching, though, that they feel so passionately connected to the land that spawned an ancestor from five generations back. A land whose owners treated them so badly that, when faced with a choice between sticking with what they knew or taking a perilous journey across the Atlantic into an unknown world, they chose the latter.

TYPE TWO
Species: *there is no type two*

After careful consideration in the bath tonight, I've realised that nobody really cares a great deal for family history, other than Americans. I'm not entirely sure why this is. Occasionally Australians or New Zealanders will make a vague inquiry, but on the whole it is American customers who seem to be obsessed by this. I don't really know why. It's not as though there's anything wrong with identifying as being American, although perhaps in a land of immigrants the only way to differentiate yourself is to cling on to a piece of the land you left, even if it is several generations behind you. As someone with an Irish mother and English father I feel slightly stateless, and as such probably identify more than I ought to with the land of my birth: Scotland. It's far simpler to answer the question 'Where are you from?' with a single word than to embark on a lengthy (and dull) explanation of your genealogy. Perhaps it would be easier if everyone, when asked that question, replied 'The Great Rift Valley.'

Bonus

CLEARLY LINNAEUS had a considerably better grasp of his system of classification than I have, as mine has failed me remarkably. I had intended to slip this genus in earlier, but—as with most elements of the way in which I conduct my business—an entirely predictable element of disorganisation has crept in, and I'm now forced to shoehorn this final chapter in under the transparently obvious pretence that it is an 'added extra.' Perhaps we ought to have called the book *Eight Types of People You Find in Bookshops*, but it's all a bit too late now—the press release has gone out—so what follows is a fudge in which I hope you'll indulge me, with my apologies.

8

Genus: *Operarii*

(STAFF)

O F ALL the types covered in this book, the only one you can guarantee will always be in a bookshop is staff. They are the interface, the front line, and the foot soldiers of the industry—and they suffer for it. Everyone has an interest in which they possess an above-average amount of knowledge, but customers tend to expect that—because you work in a bookshop—you should know as much as they do about, for example, the life of William Makepeace Thackeray. An eighteen-year-old medical student who works part-time in Waterstones could not reasonably be expected to know that Thackeray's wife—suffering from depression—attempted to take her own life by jumping from a ferry on a journey between Anglesey and Dún Laoghaire but failed in her efforts because her crinoline skirt acted like a balloon and left her floating in the Irish Sea while the vessel turned around to rescue her. Nonetheless, the Thackeray expert will delight in exposing her ignorance, despite knowing considerably less than she about, for example, the endocrine function of the islets of Langerhans in the pancreas.

I should qualify this by pointing out that the first three types in this category are mainly found only in shops selling new books. Sadly, the world of second-hand books is largely populated by people who own and run their own businesses and—with a few exceptions—can't afford the luxury of staff. Student Hugo is possibly the only exception to this rule, and—like the Colossus of Rhodes—bestrides the two sides of the business, thankfully (mostly) not naked, and never urinating into the Aegean Sea.

TYPE ONE
Species: *discipulus hugo*
(STUDENT HUGO)

Student Hugo is the bookshop owner's father's aunt's cousin (or something), and is in his final year at university. His branch of the family has done remarkably better than the owner of the bookshop's line, but some sadist among them—a bored parent or vindictive godmother—has decided that spending a summer working in a bookshop would teach young Hugo a valuable lesson. The lesson being, presumably, that working in a bookshop is a singularly terrible idea. Nobody on the bookshop owner's side of the family quite knows who Hugo is, but there's some sort of genetic connection which, on meeting him, the owner of the bookshop will inevitably be considerably less than delighted to discover. He never stops grinning, thinks that Toulouse-Lautrec is a French rugby club and is the eldest son of a *pantalon rouge*. Following his six-month sojourn in the bookshop (during which he will have comprehensively failed to endear himself to a single other member of the staff, and proved to be of absolutely no help to even a solitary customer), he will be fast-tracked to a position in Lloyd's of London due entirely to the fact that Great Aunt Spanky (real name Anne) has considerable influence. Once there, he will spend the rest of his working life lazily making appalling financial decisions with other people's money, for which he will be richly rewarded. At university, he is doing his finals in Grouse Studies following the advice of Uncle Pongo (real name Rupert), who told him to pick the course with the fewest hours, which, by an entirely unsurprising coincidence, was also the course that required the most pitiful A-level results. Despite all of this, student Hugo is an affable type: kind and generous too. If you want to hear the most accurate portrayal of student Hugo, you can do no better than to listen to Marcus Brigstocke's superb radio series *Giles Wemmbley-Hogg Goes Off.*

TYPE TWO

Species: *discipula maria*

(STUDENT MARY)

Student Mary is also in the shop during breaks from university, the difference being that she is there because she needs the money and is passionate about literature. Unlike student Hugo, she will be able to answer almost any customer's question. Student Mary's passion for the written word has led her to embark on an ill-advised MA in literature, focusing on 'The Impact of Male Death on William Faulkner's Female Characters, 1929 to 1936' or something similar, thus ensuring that her academic excellence will never translate into a lucrative career. While student Hugo's mind is rarely troubled by even the smallest cirrostratus cloud of original thought, and is consequently incapable of contemplating the notion of failure (despite an overwhelming body of evidence), student Mary's is a dense fog of self-doubt and lack of confidence. As a consequence, in spite of her vastly superior intellect, she always skulks in student Hugo's shadow, spending her days in the back room, sorting through boxes of books and avoiding the public wherever possible, while student Hugo is front-of-shop boring trapped customers about the demise of the grouse populations of Dartmoor. Despite her shyness, student Mary is not unhelpful, but will only share her knowledge if repeatedly asked to do so by a customer, and even then with meek embarrassment.

TYPE THREE

Species: *stultus cum barba*

(HIPSTER)

These abominable creatures have only one redeeming feature, and that is that they believe that books are cool, in the same way that they believe that vinyl, tweed and beards are cool. Which, of course, they are, but because they always have been rather cool, and not because they have become the sartorial essentials of a pseudo-nerdy countercultural uniform. I'm reluctant to credit the hipster with anything else, because they're deeply irritating in almost every other way, and have jumped on a bandwagon which makes even goths look like they're outlandishly individual. They're easily identified in the outside world because they can usually be seen in a café reading Baudelaire (a tattered, second-hand paperback copy which gives the illusion both that they're re-reading it and that they are impoverished intellectuals) through a thick pair of 1970s NHS glasses which they bought for £200 from some bloke in a market stall in Camden who told them that they'd been worn by Tom Lehrer during his live performance of 'The Elements' in Copenhagen in 1967. But the hipster never turns the page because they're not actually reading the book. Rather, it is—like their beard, their glasses, and their pipe—something to be seen with.

In the bookshop where they work, the hipster is the diametric opposite of student Mary—they are there to be visible and aloof, unhelpful and resentful of any interruption to their vital work of feigning a look of melancholy while staring into the middle distance over an open book and stroking their beard. Any interruption to this process by a customer will result in a four-second pause, followed by a slow turn (and tilt) of the head, a sneer down their nose over the top of Tom Lehrer's glasses and a supercilious 'Hmmm?' all of which are calculated to put the customer at such unease that they'll apologise immediately and leave the hipster to shoot one final look of disapproval on the basis that this customer may have eaten meat at some point in the past ten years.

TYPE FOUR

Species: *venditor librorum antiquorum*

(SECOND-HAND BOOKSELLER)

Ancient, crumbling and often drunk or hungover, the second-hand bookseller is self-employed for no other reason than that they have no choice. Nobody in their right mind would ever give a job to someone so completely devoid of the most rudimentary social skills that even a Neanderthal outcast would look like Jay Gatsby in their company. They share several things in common with the hipster, but through accident rather than design. They wear tweed (but because it's warm, rather than because it's fashionable). They smoke pipes (because they're proper smokers, rather than because it's fashionable). They love real books (because they're not connected to the internet, rather than because it's fashionable), and they exude a complete contempt for their customers (because it's an inevitable consequence of years of working in the trade, rather than because it is fashionable). The second-hand bookseller has been in the trade for so long that they can no longer remember how they fell into it. Perhaps it was their first job, back in the days when there was a decent living to be made in selling old books, and before long they became so comfortable with the dusty surroundings of their environment and their kindly, aged employer, that when he offered to sell them the business they jumped at the opportunity. Nobody really knows. The late Sue Townsend, in her wonderful *Adrian Mole: The Prostrate Years*, describes just such a character, Bernard Hopkins (although he is a member of staff rather than the benign owner, Mr Carlton-Hayes):

Bernard Hopkins is the bookseller from hell. If he applies for a job at Waterstones his name triggers an alarm on their computer network. At one time Borders had a photograph of him up in their staff rooms with a notice saying: 'Do not employ this man.' But there is nobody to touch him when it comes to antiquarian books. He handles them with reverence and will not sell them to a careless owner—a bit like those women at Cats Protection who require you to have a degree in cat care before they will allow you to take one home.

Bernard Hopkins is almost like a composite of every second-hand bookseller I've ever met, and his reticence in dealing with the book-buying public has nothing to do with a desire to look cool. If he'd ever had that wish, he would never have become a second-hand bookseller. Rather, it comes from nothing more than world-weariness. Once, he had enthusiasm for answering the questions of customers, but forty years of being asked—among others—the same twelve questions every day of every week, have reduced him to the belligerent wreck which he has become. Those twelve questions are as follows:

1. 'Do you get your books for free?'
2. 'How many books do you have?'
3. 'Have you read all of them?'
4. 'Can you recommend a book for my wife?' (Yes, Flaubert's *Madame Bovary* or D. H. Lawrence's *Lady Chatterley's Lover*)
5. 'Can you recommend a book for my husband?' (Yes, *The End of the Affair,* by Graham Greene)
6. 'What's the oldest book in the shop?'
7. 'What's the most expensive book in the shop?'
8. 'Why is this book £6 when it was 2 shillings when it was first published?'
9. 'Are you seriously asking £3 for this old book?'
10. 'Do I get a bulk discount if I buy two books?'
11. 'Can I bring my dog in? He's very friendly.' (The dog will immediately either urinate on the floor or start barking maniacally.)
12. 'Do you want to buy these books?' (immediately thrusts an Iceland bag full of old copies of *Take a Break* magazine over the counter, almost knocking you out)

TYPE FIVE

Species: *dominus*

(MANAGER)

Smartly dressed, clean, punctual, enthusiastic and armed with the inexplicable conviction that the customer is always right, the manager really has no place in a second-hand bookshop. Which is perhaps why you only ever find them in shops selling new books, and even then mainly in chains. The only exception to this extraordinary behaviour that I can think of to this is a story told to me by a friend who worked in a well-known Edinburgh bookshop when she was a student. My friend—a shop floor worker who was busy trying to put a Christmas window display together—had been dragged from her chore by an elderly twin-set-and-pearls Morningside woman who had demanded a copy of an out-of-print translation of *The Count of Monte Cristo*. After twenty minutes of trying to explain that it was no longer available as a new book, and that there was no way she could locate a copy, that she was busy and that there were other members of staff who could help her, the customer continued haughtily to demand it. My friend's otherwise impossibly stoic patience snapped and she told the elderly customer, 'Oh, why don't you just fuck off!' The horrified customer demanded to see the manager, and my trembling friend took her to the manager's office on the top floor of the building, expecting the worst. As the lift doors opened, she looked nervously at the manager who—it later transpired—was in the middle of dealing with several missed orders, and a few absent staff, and was not in the best of moods. She introduced the elderly woman, and—in the almost certain expectation that she would never work in the shop again—told the manager that the woman had demanded to speak to him. The twin-set-and-pearls raised herself to her full height and said, 'This wee lassie, one of your members of staff, has just told me to fuck off.' The manager, according to my friend, turned distractedly to her and said to the elderly woman—with impeccable politeness of tone—'Then why haven't you fucked off?'

Genus: *Cliens perfectus*
(PERFECT CUSTOMER)

THE PERFECT Customer is, sadly, now almost a distant memory—someone for whom a day spent in a second-hand bookshop was a day well spent. Someone who understood that for the price of a pound of paper they could lose themselves in the worlds of the imaginations of H. Rider Haggard, George Eliot or Jane Austen—worlds that took the mind of a genius to create and in which they could immerse themselves and forget about their worries for a week, and all for the cost of a cup of coffee. They're mostly gone, now, replaced by the Amazon generation, for whom the chase has no thrill, and the pound of paper's value is a penny.

When I bought the shop, the previous owner told me that things go in cycles: that twenty years before I took over there were voracious collectors of first editions of the best-known authors of their generation—J. B. Priestley, George Bernard Shaw, Jean Plaidy, Arnold Bennett. These, he assured me, had been his perfect customers, but he warned me that over the period of his tenure of the shop their numbers had dwindled, and that books which he could easily have expected to sell quickly for £20 were now gathering dust, untouched, priced at £4. But the nature of a cycle means that, as one generation dies off, another—hopefully—replaces it. And there are always authors who defy the limits of their age: Buchan, Stevenson, Ian Fleming, even Rider Haggard, still seem to sell well. It's hard to know who among the great names of contemporary literature will slowly fade away from the appetites of voracious collectors and who will stand the test of time. Of course, rare editions of all of these authors still appeal to collectors but, increasingly, those people are becoming fewer and farther between. In 200 years will Hilary Mantel, Ian McEwan, Julian Barnes and other giants of our age be elevated into literary immortality or almost forgotten? It's impossible to know how kindly time will judge any of us. Will J. K. Rowling or Margaret Atwood become the Jane Austen of our times or end up as footnotes in a literary journal? Will Donna Tartt's extraordinary, epic novels be read with the same reverence as Tolstoy, Homer and Hardy? Who knows whether the genius of Alan Bennett's astute social observations will still be as relevant when viewed through the lens of a reader a century from now?

TYPE ONE

Species: *homo qui libros litterarios colligit*
(FICTION COLLECTOR)

So much fiction has been published over the years that our meagre stock of about 2,000 novels barely scratches the surface, so it's extremely rare that we'll have the book that the fiction collector is looking for. When we do, though, their delight is palpable. In most cases, it's a title that they've spent a considerable number of years hunting down. They generally don't use online search engines and have the dogged determination of the past generation of customers, for whom the internet wasn't an option. It's normally something scarce, or a specific edition, and there's never any 'negotiation' on the price.

TYPE TWO

Species: *homo qui libros de via ferrata colligit*
(RAILWAY COLLECTOR)

Like others, this is a type whose existence I have praised in previous books. The railway collector is a species unlike all others, and whose passion is as fiery as their dress sense is bland. For them, the holy grail of literature is anything on the subject of the steam rolling stock of the LNER, or the collectable nameplates of the Victorian trains of the London, Brighton & South Coast Railway. If you have what they're looking for, they will treat you like a lord.

TYPE THREE

Species: *homines normales*
(NORMAL PEOPLE)

This is a type so rare that to categorise them as normal people seems somewhat of a misnomer. They don't always know what they're looking for and—as such—could easily fall into the monstrous regiment of vaguely curious time-wasters, but they're different in as much as they know they want something for themselves but are sufficiently open-minded not to have a specific title in mind. They always leave the shop with something. And their most endearing quality is—like every other perfect customer—that they will happily pay the asking price without forcing you to engage in a mutually humiliating public argument about it.

TYPE FOUR
Species: *de scientia scripta fanaticus*
(SCI-FI FAN)

I doubt whether there's a single bookseller who will ever tell you that they have anything but the purest of love for the sci-fi fan. The same can be said of the graphic novel collector. Some of the giants of literature have contributed to the former genre: Doris Lessing, J. G. Ballard, H. G. Wells, Mary Shelley, Iain M. Banks, Ursula Le Guin, George Orwell, Aldous Huxley and P. D. James all tried their hands at it, and Douglas Adams too, to name but a handful. When I was in my teens, I was obsessed with Harry Harrison's *Stainless Steel Rat* series, and Kurt Vonnegut's *Cat's Cradle*, in which ice-nine, a government manufactured chemical weapon, turns everyone (and everything) who touches it to ice. It seems strangely prescient as I write this and the virus has shut most of the planet down.

Over the years I've bought several sci-fi collections,

all of which have flown from the shelves the moment the word gets round that they're in the shop. Collectors know one another, and when I tell one of them that I've acquired a library, they flock to the shop in their droves. Aside from the Asimov and Bradbury buyers, this type also attracts illustrator collectors. Sci-fi paperbacks (and they're mostly first published in paperback) tend to have the most extraordinarily lurid and stylishly illustrated covers. I suspect that the publishers have insisted that the illustrators spend at least a week on a mind-bending daily dose of LSD before putting brush to paper in most, if not all, cases.

The sci-fi fan is instantly recognisable. To say that they are social misfits would be to do them a huge disservice. They fit in, but they only ever want to do so on their own terms, and in the comfort of their own community. They are a clan, and identify in the same way that the *pantalons rouges* club together. As a bookseller, the joy of the sci-fi fan is that they're never disappointed. Provided you have something in stock by Philip K. Dick, or anything with a cover illustration by Joseph Mugnaini, they will be delighted. There is a uniform, of course. It usually involves a T-shirt (black) with either a *Star Wars* or a *Dr Who* retro design. Shoes (trainers) are a mandatory white. Endearingly, the sci-fi fan is never alone: they always come in pairs, and usually as a charmingly—if tiresomely—infatuated couple. And always wearing identical clothes. Somehow they manage to pull off the seemingly impossible feat of being simultaneously less cool yet more cool than the hipster.

The graphic novel fan is cut from similar cloth, although of a marginally lighter shade of black. The graphic novel has in recent years risen from the gutter of literary criticism to be now deservedly squinting in surprise at the stars. In 2018 Nick Drnaso's *Sabrina* was long listed for the Booker Prize. Art Spiegelman's *Maus* and Neil Gaiman's *Sandman* deserve equal, if not greater, recognition as works of literary excellence. The graphic novel fan is similar in appearance to the sci-fi fan, but is of a far more earnest disposition. It's rare for me, when buying books, to come across graphic novels, but when I do, I usually find them in considerable numbers. And when buyers come in looking for them, they usually buy them in equally large quantities.

WITHOUT LOVERS of books, I would have no business, so I should conclude with an apology, and in words far more articulate than my own. Roy Harley Lewis ends his *Antiquarian Books* with this:

'Most other enthusiasts, whether they are propagating religion, politics, or even sport, seem to be fired by a crusading spirit. But the lover of anti-quarian books feels he has something in common with other bibliophiles. Crusaders are invariably thoroughly irritating, so forget about soapboxes. I am talking not even about a 'soft sell' but more about a discreet word here and a sharing of excitement there. A public more aware of antiquarian books can only stimulate the trade, and that is all anyone can ask.'

A NOTE ON THE TYPE

Our text is set in Granjon. This typeface is named in honor of Robert Granjon. He was the boldest and most original designer in his day. Between 1557 and 1562 Granjon printed about twenty books in types designed by himself.

However, it's neither a copy of a classic face nor an entirely original creation. George W. Jones 1924 Linotype revival of Granjon is actually closer in style to the original Garamond cuts. What holds true is the most pleasant and readable italic. Robert Granjon often set his own books inspired by the cursive handwriting fashionable of his time.

Book design by Brooke Koven

1970–2020
David R. Godine
Publisher
FIFTY YEARS